GW01085576

A Purim Story

by Linda Davis

illustrated by Y. E. Taub

FELDHEIM PUBLISHERS

Jerusalem □ New York

In loving memory of
פרומע-מירל ע״ה
Florence Covell
whose birthday was Purim

Philipp Feldheim, Inc., 200 Airport Executive Park
Spring Valley, NY 10977

Feldheim Publishers Ltd. POB 6525 / Jerusalem, Israel
Printed in Israel

THE CHILDREN were restless: they scowled at the snow;
They whined and they quarreled and wished it would go;
"It's been ever so long since we last built a sukkah,
And it's almost a year until next Chanukah.
Tu B'Shvat it was hard to plant trees in the ice!
Now if Pesach came sooner, *that* would be nice…"

Then in walked their father; he listened and said,
"Purim is coming, so why don't you get
Your costumes and graggers, 'cause soon we'll fulfill a
Mitzvah when all of us hear the Megillah.

"The story took place a long time ago,
We read it each year, so that each Jew will know.
In a country called Persia — now known as Iran,
A queen wouldn't appear and the trouble began…

"You see, King Achashverosh (can *you* say his name?)
Gave a big dinner party; the whole kingdom came
From all of the provinces where the King reigned,
To his palace in Shushan, and there they remained.
And after they'd feasted on good food and wine,
The King, very pleased, said, 'This party is fine.
I'll summon Queen Vashti to put on a show.'
But when Vashti was called, her answer was 'No!'

"She refused to show up and be seen by the guests.
The angry King roared, 'She refused my request!'
His advisers advised, 'Put an end to her life.
We'll find you a Queen who will be a good wife.
We'll gather the loveliest girls ever seen,
And you shall decide who will be the next Queen.'

"In Shushan lived Mordechai, good Jewish man,
Whose cousin Hadassah was prettier than
All of the others; and when the King saw her,
There was hardly a thing he wouldn't do for her.
They called her Queen Esther; the kingdom rejoiced;
And King Achashverosh was pleased with his choice.

"But Esther kept secret that she was a Jew,
For that was what Mordechai told her to do.
One day, Mordechai, sitting by the King's gate,
Overheard two men plotting to assassinate

Achashverosh. He told Esther, 'Go warn the King!'
So the two villains failed to accomplish a thing.
And in the King's books, these events were recorded,
Although Mordechai was never rewarded.

"Now trouble arose for the Jews of Shushan:
The King's wicked minister, known as Haman,
Ordered that each man bow down to the ground,
And glorify Haman when he was around.

"But Mordechai would not bow down to Haman.
'Jews worship no man, only God, Who is One.'
Furious, Haman cried, 'Since he refused,
I'll tell Achashverosh to kill all the Jews!
I will first choose a day for the deed to be done,
By throwing a *pur*,' said the evil Haman.

"(He used to throw *pur* — just like dice in a game;
And that is how *Purim* acquired its name.)
'The day that comes up is the date we will use
To kill Mordechai and the rest of the Jews.'
So he went to the King; Achashverosh agreed;
The thirteenth of Adar was the day they decreed.

"All the Jews would be killed — every one in Iran.
Mordechai tore his clothes when he learned of the plan,
And in sackcloth and ashes, sat by the King's gate,
To warn his good cousin, the Queen, of their fate.
Perturbed and distressed, good Queen Esther then said,
'I must help them out, though I might wind up dead.'

" (For though she was Queen, Esther never forgot,
That she was a Jew, and their *pur* was her lot.)
'Tell the Jews,' said Queen Esther, 'not to eat — not a thing! —
For three days and three nights, then I'll plead with the King.'

"Meanwhile, one night, when the King could not sleep,
He asked for the history books that kings keep.
He read there how Mordechai warned of a plot,
Had he been rewarded? Oh, no! He had not!
So the King asked himself, 'Now what should we do
To honor a man who's so loyal and true?'

"At that very moment, someone knocked at the door.
'Twas none other than Haman who'd come to ask for
The King's royal permission to hang Mordechai
High on a gallows that reached toward the sky.
But first the King asked him, 'What would *you* do
To honor a man who's been loyal and true?'
Not having heard what had been said before,
Haman thought it was *he* whom the honors were for.

" 'Let him wear the King's robes! Ride his horse! Wear his crown!
Have a servant announce as he's led through the town,
"The King's friends are honored in this special way!" '
Achashverosh agreed, 'We'll do as you say
For the Jew Mordechai who sits at my gate!'
Haman burned up with rage, for his envy was great.

"Then Esther made feasts for Haman and the King;
Achashverosh was pleased, and said 'most anything
That she asked would be granted. So Esther's request was
That her life be spared and the lives of the rest of
The Jews in the kingdom. The King was dismayed
When he realized what terrible plans he'd okayed.

"Enraged, the King left, but returned to the scene,
And thought he saw Haman attacking the Queen!
Thus all Haman's schemes were disrupted that day,
As the royal guards grabbed him and dragged him away.
To the very same gallows which he had constructed
To hang Mordechai, he himself was conducted.

" 'Mordechai,' said the King, 'you have my consent;
Inform all your people that they may defend
Themselves from their enemies. Here, take my ring.
They'll know that these orders came straight from the King.'

"And the King, realizing that no one was wiser,
Made Mordechai act as his Royal Adviser.
'On Adar the thirteenth, let the Jews take up swords
And kill all their foes, be they peasants or lords.'
In Shushan the Jews received extra permission
To fight on Adar the fourteenth in addition.

"Soon it was over, the fighting all through;
Haman's ten evil sons were killed and hanged too.
With feasting and gladness, the Jews celebrated;
Thus was the holiday Purim created.

"Ever since then, the fourteenth of Adar
Is a day of rejoicing for Jews near and far;
But Adar the fifteenth is when Purim falls
In Jerusalem, Shushan and cities with walls.

"To celebrate Purim, four mitzvos we do:
The Megillah we read (or we hear) two times through;
We enjoy a great feast, and everyone sends
Tzedakah to the poor, gifts of food to our friends.

"And that, my dear children, is how this book ends."